Paris 2024

80 pages of awesome activities such as word-searches, crosswords, colouring, dot to dot word scramble, quizzes and more!

Welcome to the exciting world of the Paris 2024 Olympics! Get ready to dive into the thrill of one of the most prestigious sporting events on the planet.

In this activity book, you'll embark on a journey filled with games, puzzles, colouring, and more, all inspired by the spirit of the 2024 Olympics.

Did you know that the Olympics date all the way back to ancient Greece, where they were held in honor of the gods?

In 2024, the city of Paris, known for its rich history, iconic landmarks, and vibrant culture, will host the Olympic Games once again.

Get ready to be inspired, entertained, and amazed by the magic of the Paris 2024 Olympics and the exciting challenges in this book, Let the games begin!

There are 206 nations competing at the Paris Olympics...

With a this years games set to have 32 sports!

Close to 10 MILLION tickets will be sold for this years games!

And a whopping 3 BILLION people watch the games worldwide!

Contents

Z	G	R	P	K	N	E	A	X	C	O	G
X	U	W	G	U	U	N	Y	A	S	U	P
T	B	U	J	E	K	J	D	L	F	X	L
V	S	L	Z	H	R	N	U	L	D	I	Y
W	U	F	R	Y	A	M	S	F	L	B	Q
T	P	B	C	G	I	U	A	Z	L	K	W
K	N	R	U	W	N	Q	F	N	W	D	M
Y	B	R	B	G	E	U	M	W	Y	Y	F
O	I	N	D	I	A	J	Q	S	E	Y	Y
U	J	P	C	K	O	L	P	U	B	C	Y
F	C	P	D	E	P	E	I	L	W	G	I
O	H	X	K	A	P	J	Y	Q	H	B	L

USA
Germany
India
Ukraine
Uganda

F	N	D	X	X	R	N	Z	A	V	K	J	A	K
C	D	Y	L	E	S	C	I	R	H	F	E	T	Y
F	U	T	M	T	X	V	M	G	V	L	R	G	O
U	L	O	J	P	L	I	M	E	E	A	T	L	B
H	Z	O	L	B	A	D	S	N	A	R	C	N	X
M	G	H	P	S	A	X	B	T	H	G	I	S	P
O	L	N	Y	H	M	E	X	I	C	O	O	A	L
J	Y	U	I	I	N	T	I	N	J	Y	X	B	Q
V	B	O	E	B	C	I	H	A	O	V	I	Z	I
O	U	R	E	G	R	D	D	X	T	F	Z	O	T
L	L	S	R	K	U	A	K	X	I	W	E	Z	Q
F	T	Q	N	B	N	E	H	F	Z	I	Q	U	G
K	D	F	Z	A	L	P	E	M	Y	G	F	K	F
Y	A	Z	C	H	I	N	A	Y	O	K	K	B	E

China
Nigeria
Mexico
Argentina
Canada

Z	A	C	O	S	B	R	Q	Q	F	I	Q	W	T	B	F
H	O	S	E	W	W	F	Z	J	J	M	Y	B	K	E	X
W	L	A	Y	Y	I	I	V	C	O	B	R	H	X	L	B
V	C	C	X	C	Y	C	T	J	Q	G	L	R	S	G	M
K	Z	V	M	D	V	E	W	Z	T	S	P	D	R	I	J
N	S	Q	Y	F	S	L	X	K	E	O	V	V	D	U	W
F	O	X	Z	M	A	A	G	V	Z	R	D	Y	G	M	T
F	I	Y	T	D	C	N	M	P	X	M	L	F	M	U	M
W	D	C	D	S	Y	D	M	W	W	A	F	A	I	H	Q
C	F	Z	M	S	H	F	F	F	T	M	N	J	N	B	J
U	R	I	Z	G	T	C	A	I	P	N	V	W	K	D	A
E	A	X	L	U	D	D	N	K	F	W	P	G	X	U	U
O	N	K	G	H	I	S	A	I	W	G	U	V	U	T	E
K	C	H	S	L	E	M	I	G	W	J	V	F	D	B	J
E	E	K	H	B	G	W	K	G	M	H	J	Y	N	B	H
G	W	V	F	D	B	G	M	Q	S	R	T	P	J	L	R

Italy
Iceland
France
Switzerland
Belgium

D	Z	Q	G	Q	P	W	A	Y	A	T	V	J
B	R	O	U	U	M	F	J	J	L	G	T	R
F	V	L	F	D	Y	C	Q	A	Y	B	K	D
U	L	H	T	V	E	D	T	F	I	L	W	P
X	Q	L	P	P	O	L	A	N	D	E	Z	Z
L	T	A	N	J	J	I	J	O	S	H	A	V
L	E	V	V	O	B	L	S	R	M	I	F	A
C	C	Q	I	R	E	Y	V	W	R	T	A	G
B	R	O	E	J	J	I	P	A	E	Z	P	B
U	D	S	V	M	L	F	G	Y	E	D	H	I
J	V	Q	Q	T	V	L	V	W	J	R	E	V
E	J	J	V	U	U	D	L	B	A	B	V	N
J	I	S	V	B	X	E	B	V	L	N	P	T

Norway
Serbia
Sweden
Bulgaria
Poland

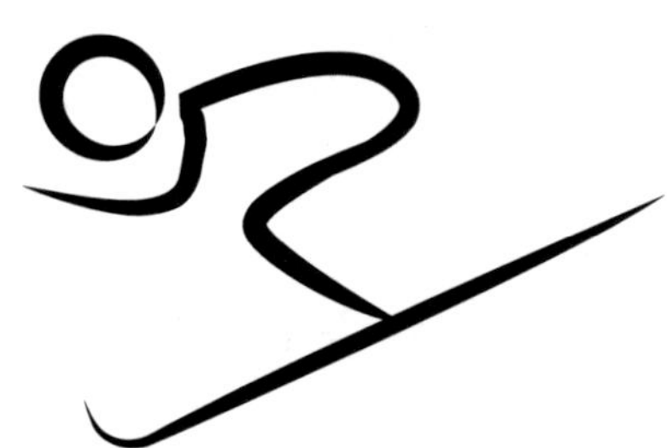

F X V N D H O M W O O J V F X
R I V C Z N H P C T P X Z V A
F Q N S R Q A R V J I D R O I
K D A L B A N I A K P N X Q T
M S T S A M N X F T J T K A V
R T L E O N G C N D O A G V N
P E P Z Y U D S I B K L R E I
O Y N H E P T P T R M C U H O
D F J G S F I H A D W O D C X
V W T E Y V O M K N U O C Y A
E E V E G Y N Y K O C O I M D
W B B V T E Y U X J R N P L R
S T I L D H I A K R O E S B A
W P O P I I N J O M I Q A N A
X T Q E O Y E M Z D A J U O D

Albania
Morocco
Finland
South Korea
Denmark

ANSWERS

Z	G	R	P	K	N	E	A	X	C	O	G
X	U	W	G	U	U	N	Y	A	S	U	P
T	B	U	J	E	K	J	D	L	F	X	L
V	S	L	Z	H	R	N	U	L	D	I	Y
W	U	F	R	Y	A	M	S	F	L	B	Q
T	P	B	C	G	I	U	A	Z	L	K	W
K	N	R	U	W	N	Q	F	N	W	D	M
Y	B	R	B	G	E	U	M	W	Y	Y	F
O	I	N	D	I	A	J	Q	S	E	Y	Y
U	J	P	C	K	O	L	P	U	B	C	Y
F	C	P	D	E	P	E	I	L	W	G	I
O	H	X	K	A	P	J	Y	Q	H	B	L

ANSWERS

F N D X X R N Z A V K J A K
C D Y L E S C I R H F E T Y
F U T M T X V M G V L R G O
U L O J P L I M E E A T L B
H Z O L B A D S N A R C N X
M G H P S A X B T H G I S P
O L N Y H M E X I C O O A L
J Y U I I N T I N J Y X B Q
V B O E B C I H A O V I Z I
O U R E G R D D X T F Z O T
L L S R K U A K X I W E Z Q
F T Q N B N E H F Z I Q U G
K D F Z A L P E M Y G F K F
Y A Z C H I N A Y O K K B E

ANSWERS

Z A C O S B R Q Q F I Q W T B F
H O S E W W F Z J J M Y B K E X
W L A Y Y I I V C O B R H X L B
V C C X C Y C T J Q G L R S G M
K Z V M D V E W Z T S P D R I J
N S Q Y F S L X K E O V V D U W
F O X Z M A A G V Z R D Y G M T
F I Y T D C N M P X M L F M U M
W D C D S Y D M W W A F A I H Q
C F Z M S H F F F T M N J N B J
U R I Z G T C A I P N V W K D A
E A X L U D D N K F W P G X U U
O N K G H I S A I W G U V U T E
K C H S L E M I G W J V F D B J
E E K H B G W K G M H J Y N B H
G W V F D B G M Q S R T P J L R

ANSWERS

D	Z	Q	G	Q	P	W	A	Y	A	T	V	J
B	R	O	U	U	M	F	J	J	L	G	T	R
F	V	L	F	D	Y	C	Q	A	Y	B	K	D
U	L	H	T	V	E	D	T	F	I	L	W	P
X	Q	L	P	P	O	L	A	N	D	E	Z	Z
L	T	A	N	J	J	I	J	O	S	H	A	V
L	E	V	V	O	B	L	S	R	M	I	F	A
C	C	Q	I	R	E	Y	V	W	R	T	A	G
B	R	O	E	J	J	I	P	A	E	Z	P	B
U	D	S	V	M	L	F	G	Y	E	D	H	I
J	V	Q	Q	T	V	L	V	W	J	R	E	V
E	J	J	V	U	U	D	L	B	A	B	V	N
J	I	S	V	B	X	E	B	V	L	N	P	T

ANSWERS

F	X	V	N	D	H	O	M	W	O	O	J	V	F	X
R	I	V	C	Z	N	H	P	C	T	P	X	Z	V	A
F	Q	N	S	R	Q	A	R	V	J	I	D	R	O	I
K	D	A	L	B	A	N	I	A	K	P	N	X	Q	T
M	S	T	S	A	M	N	X	F	T	J	T	K	A	V
R	T	L	E	O	N	G	C	N	D	O	A	G	V	N
P	E	P	Z	Y	U	D	S	I	B	K	L	R	E	I
O	Y	N	H	E	P	T	P	T	R	M	C	U	H	O
D	F	J	G	S	F	I	H	A	D	W	O	D	C	X
V	W	T	E	Y	V	O	M	K	N	U	O	C	Y	A
E	E	V	E	G	Y	N	Y	K	O	C	O	I	M	D
W	B	B	V	T	E	Y	U	X	J	R	N	P	L	R
S	T	I	L	D	H	I	A	K	R	O	E	S	B	A
W	P	O	P	I	I	N	J	O	M	I	Q	A	N	A
X	T	Q	E	O	Y	E	M	Z	D	A	J	U	O	D

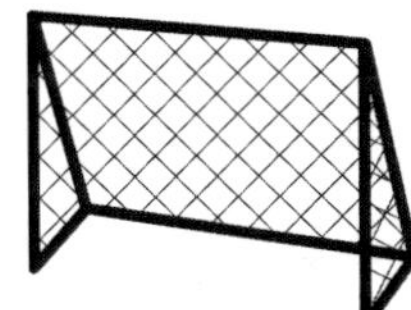

M5

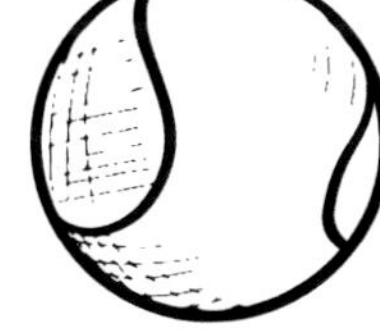

ANSWERS

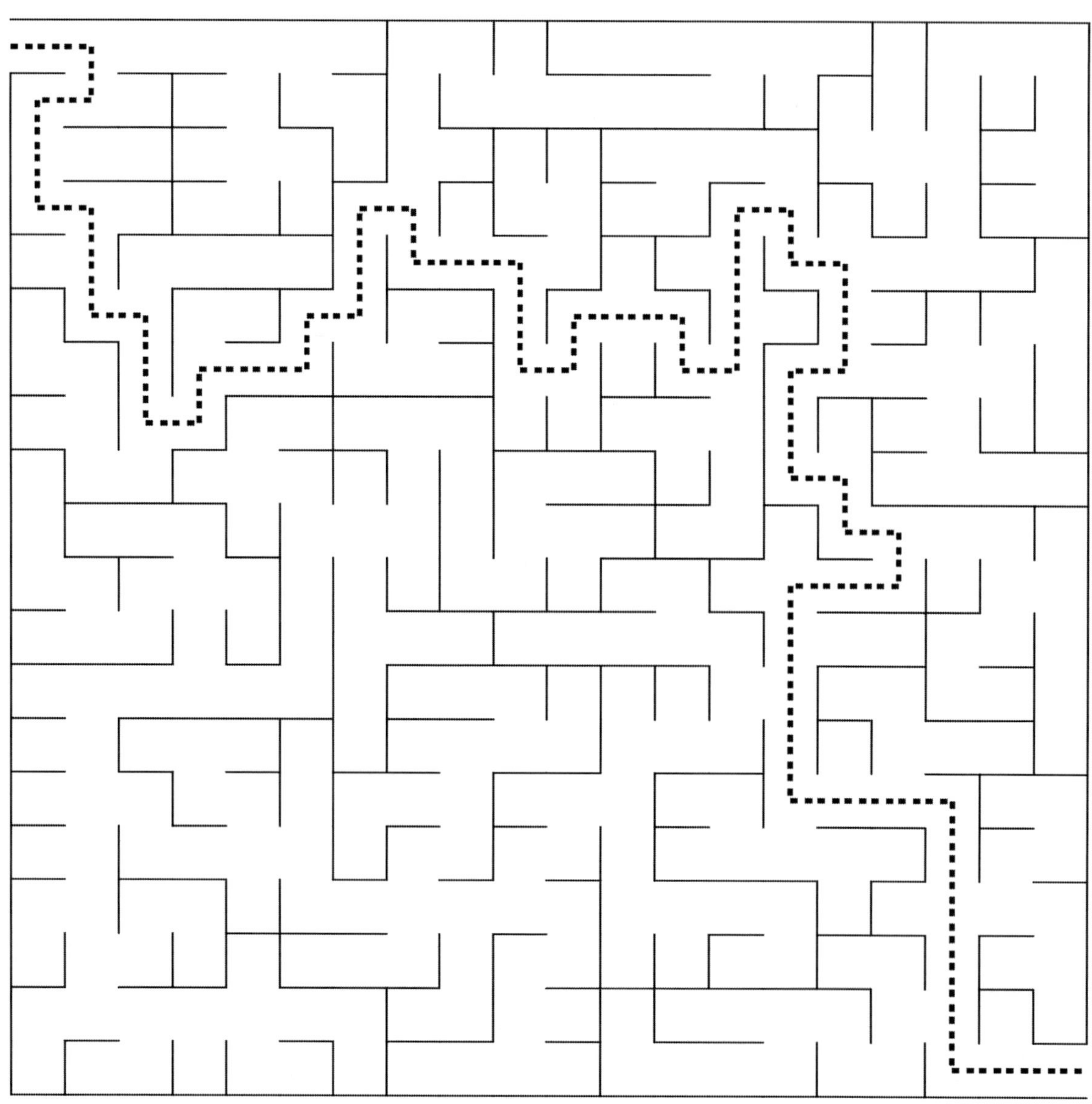

ANSWERS

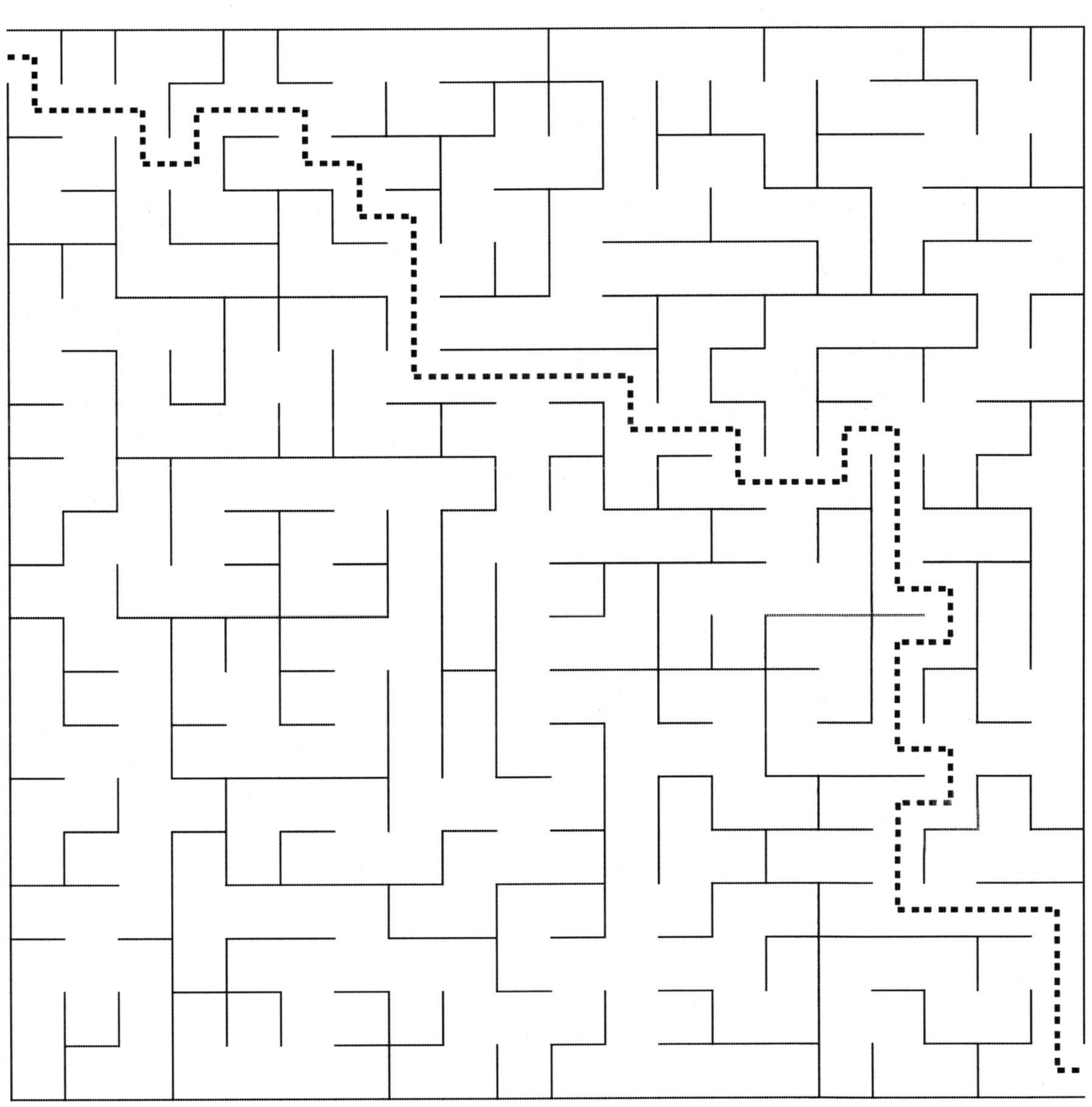

ANSWERS

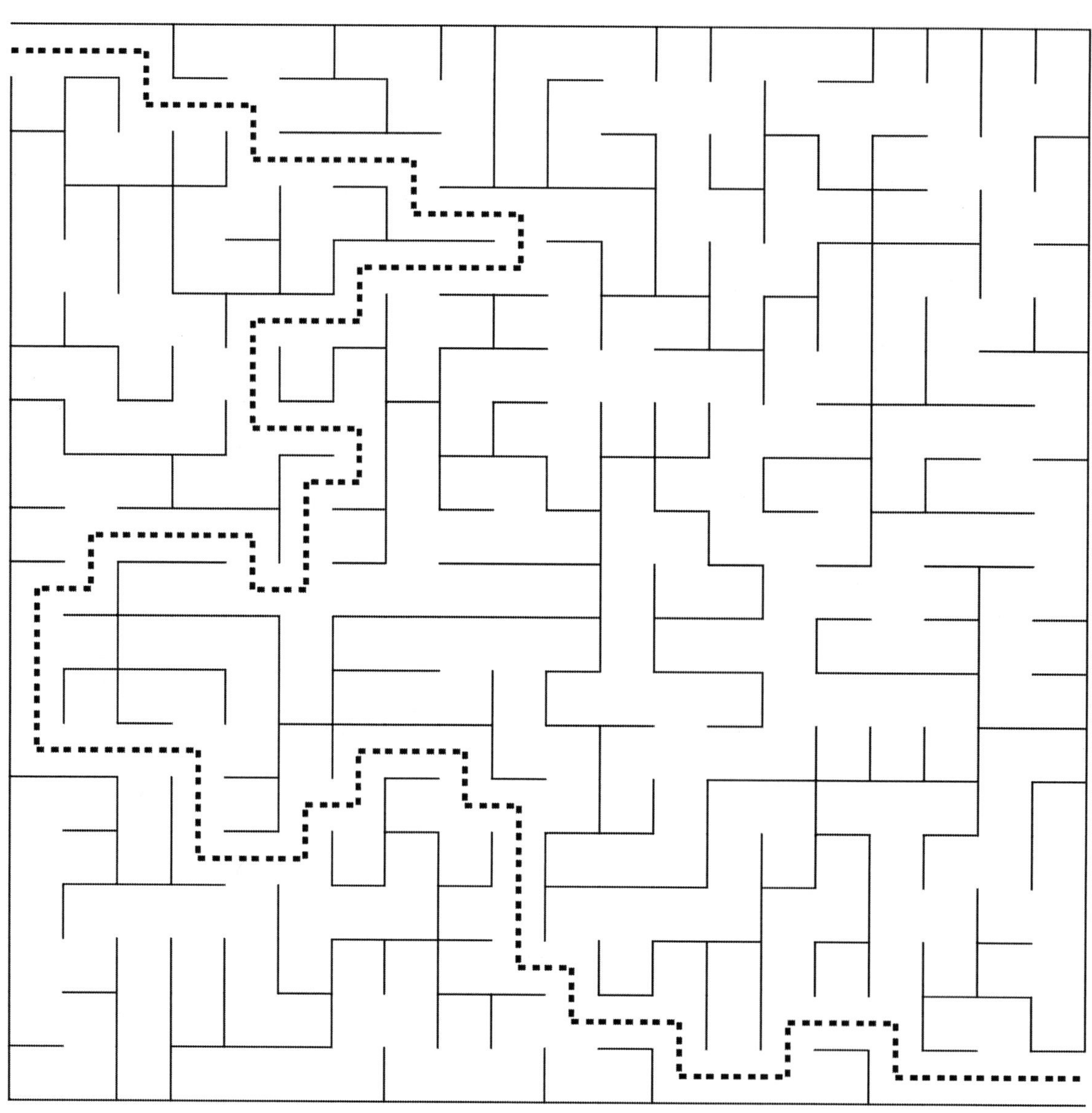

ANSWERS

M4

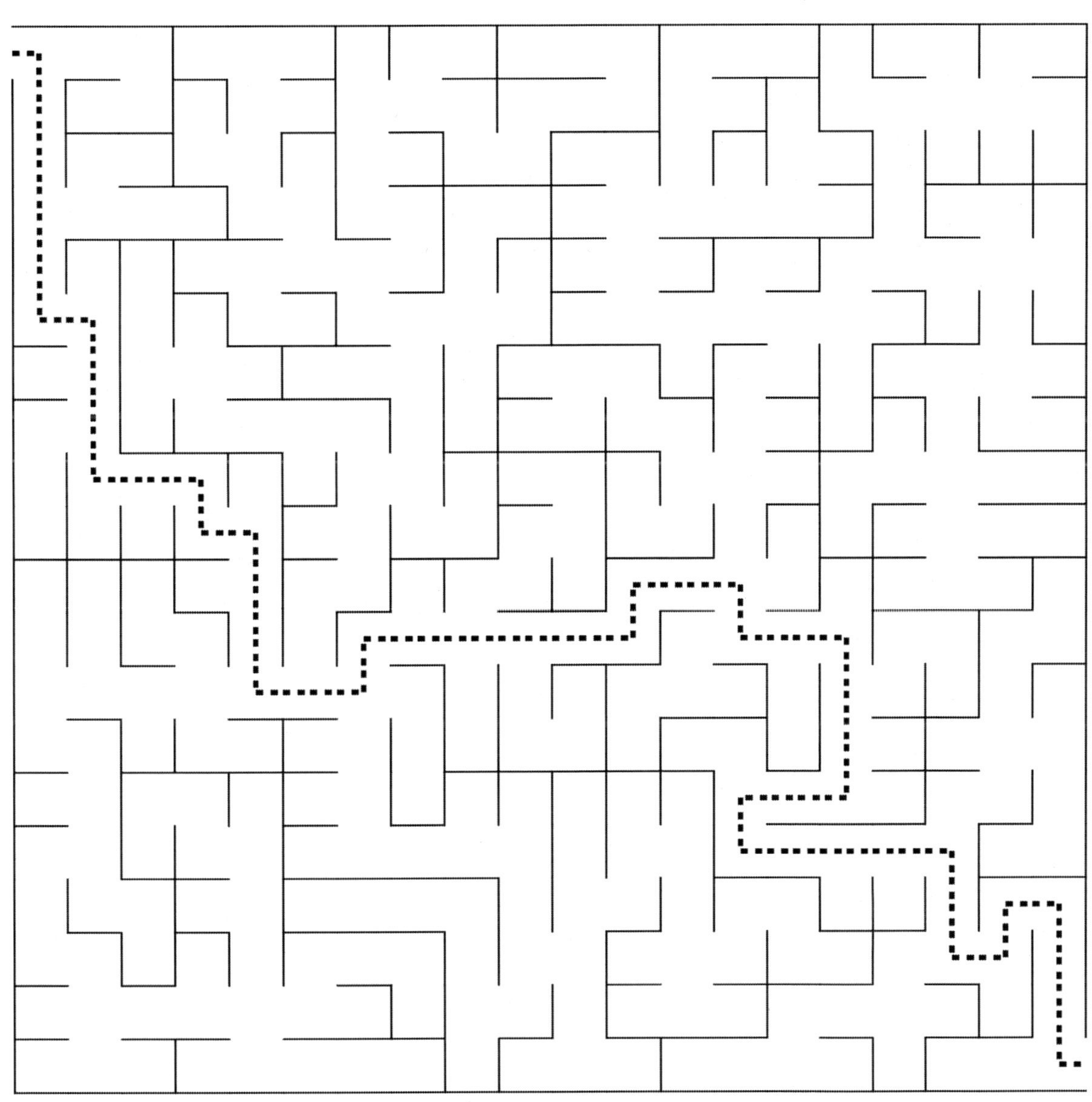

ANSWERS

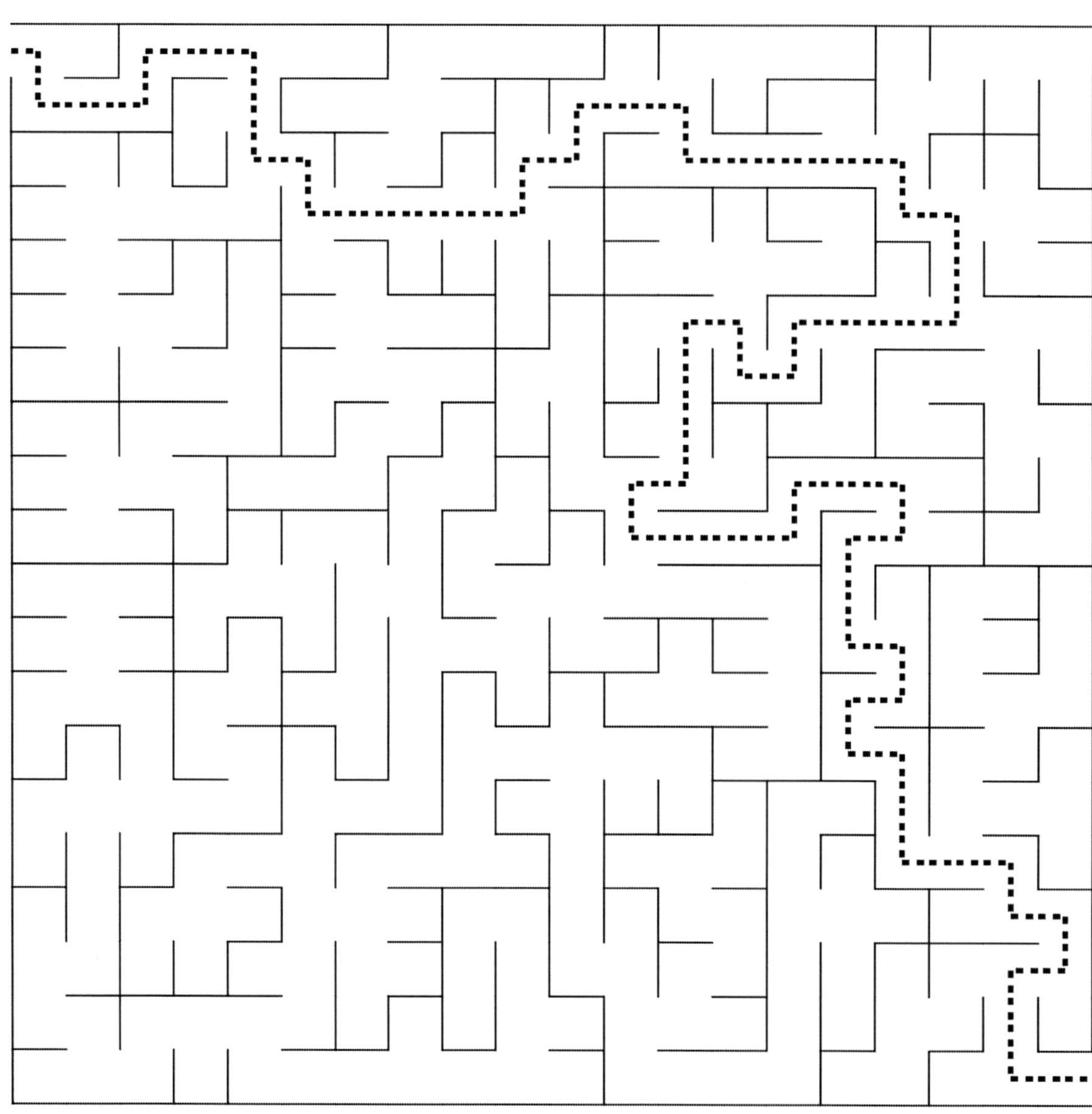

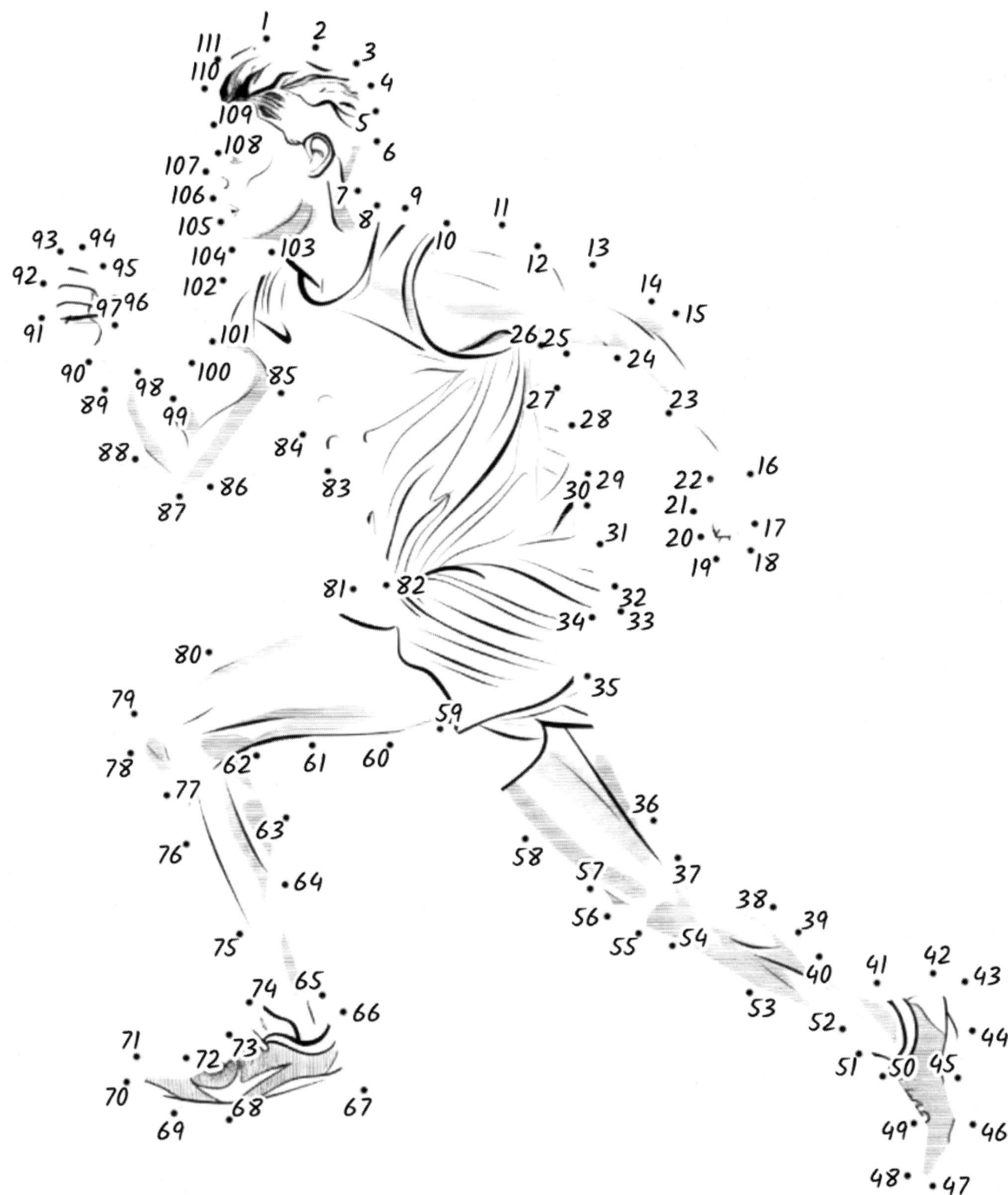

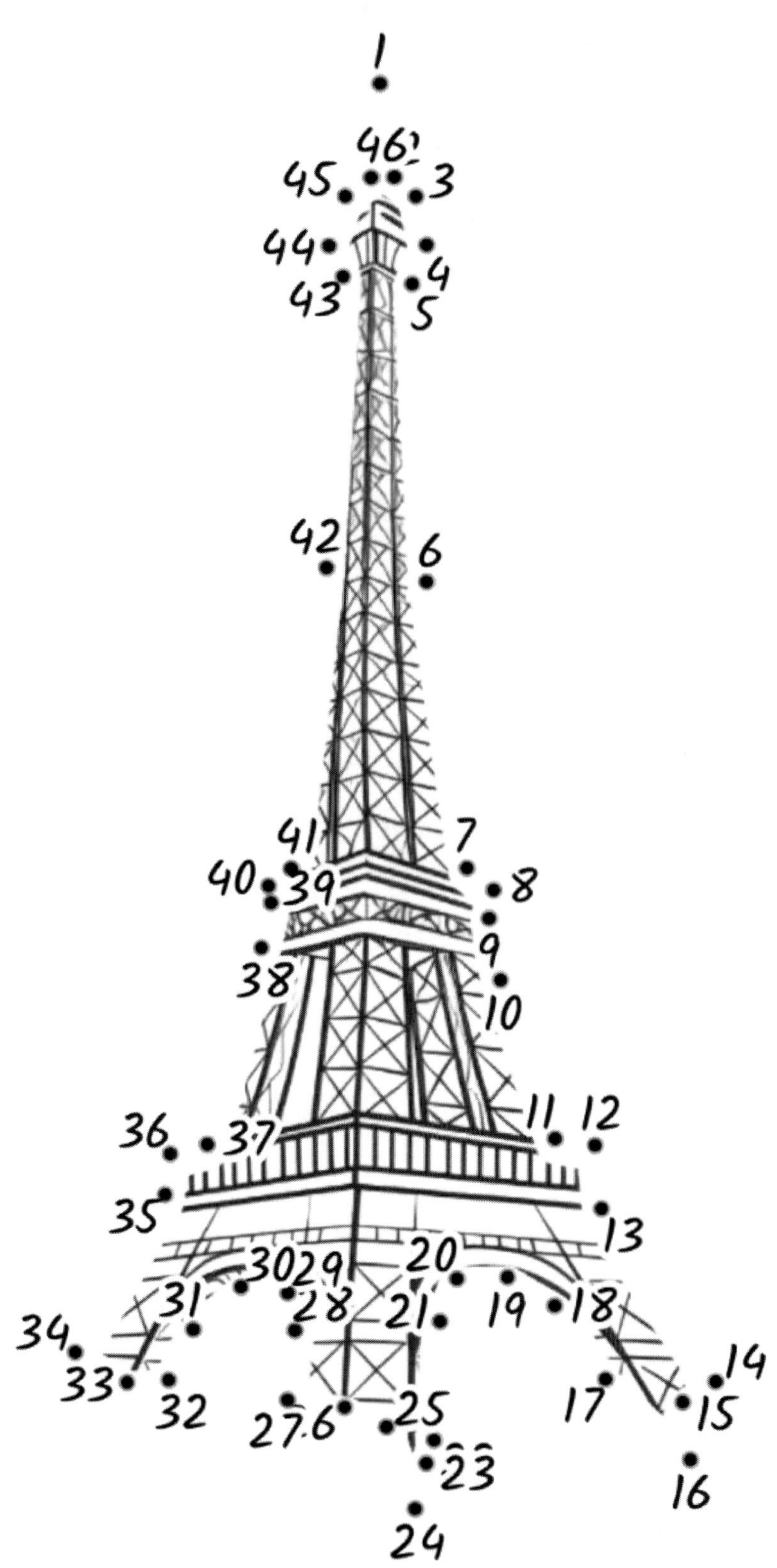

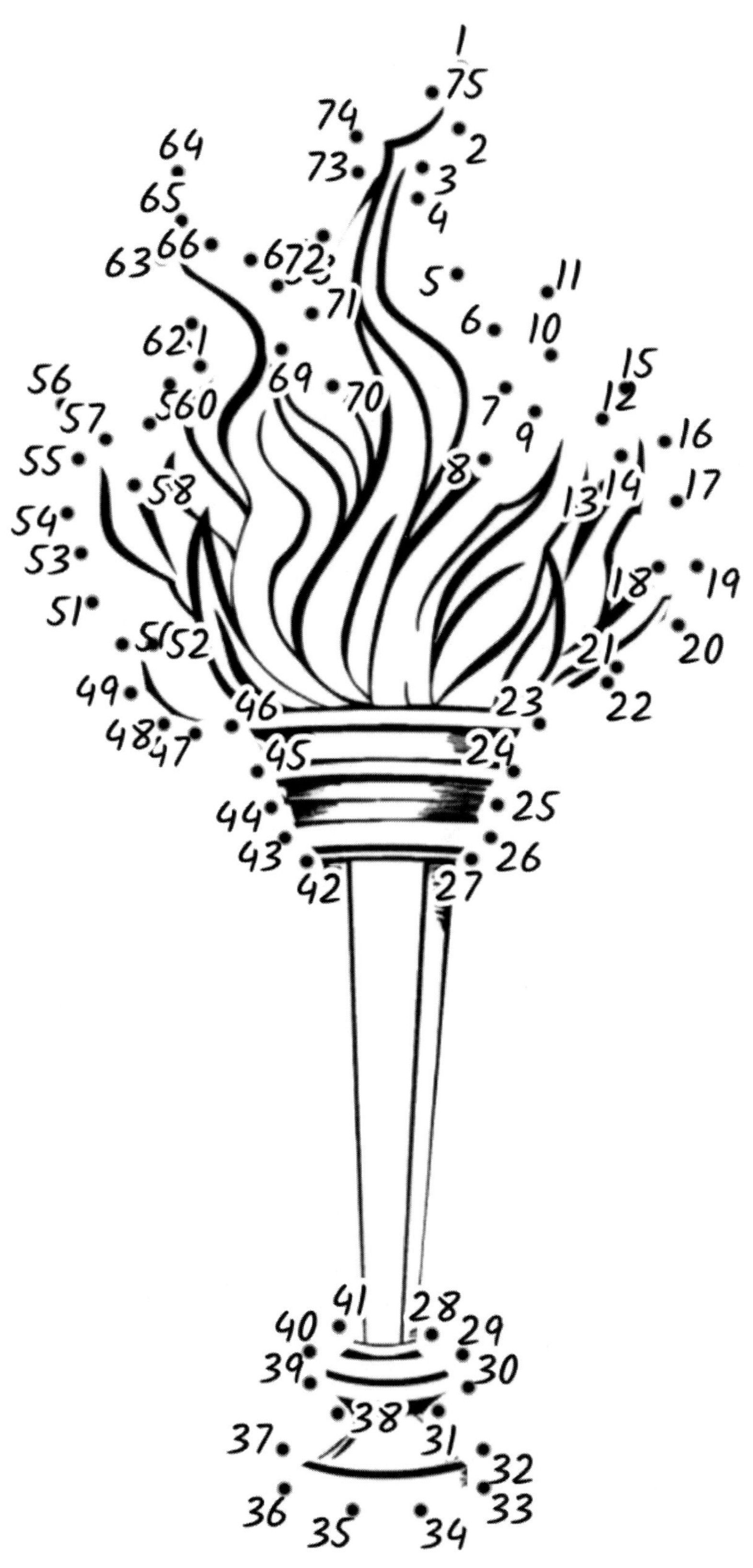

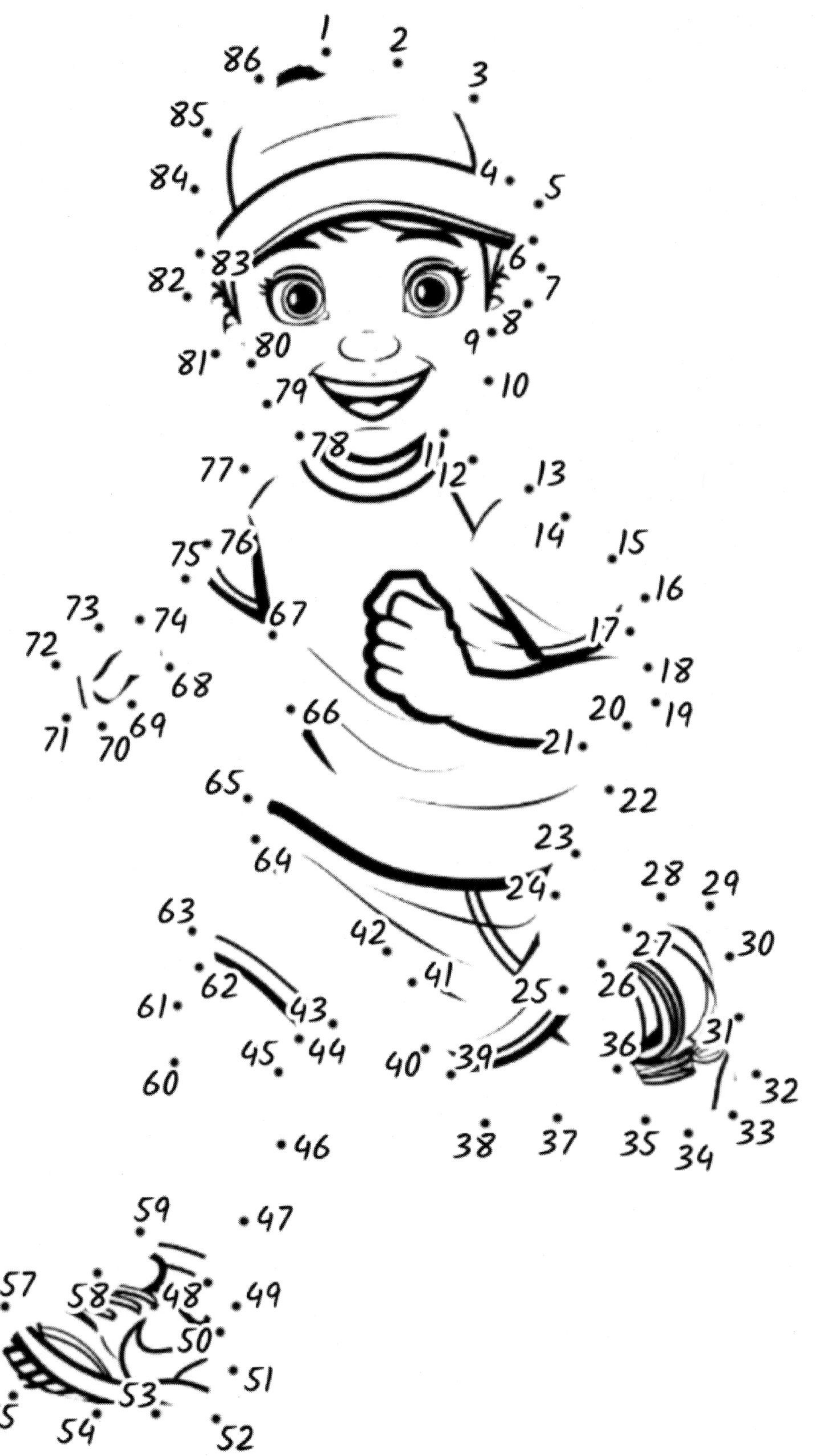

Across:

1.Players use sticks to hit a ball or puck into the opponents goal.

2.Players attempt to hit a ball and run around a series of bases to score runs.

3.A water sport where participants ride waves while standing or lying on a board.

Down:

4. A Korean martial art and Olympic sport with an emphasis on kicking techniques.

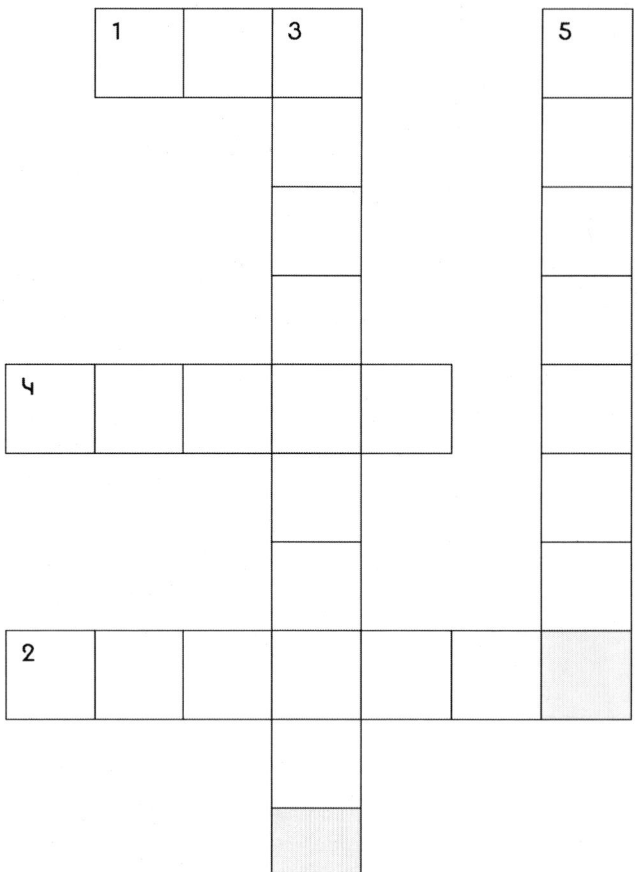

Across:

1.A country with the NFL, MLB and MLS sporting leagues.

2.In this country you may get snails served as food in restaurants.

4.This countries flag features red and gold colours.

Down:

3.This country are the latest winners of the FIFA World Cup.

5.The hamburger originated from this nation.

Across:

4.A sport where athletes spring into water, while performing acrobatic movements.

5.A multi-sport race that typically includes swimming, cycling and running.

Down:

1.A sport where athletes compete to lift the heaviest weights possible.

2.The sport of navigating a boat or ship across water using the power of wind.

3.A sport that involves performing routines requiring physical strength, flexibility & balance.

Across:

3.A sport involving the use of firearms or airguns to hit targets from varying distances.

4.A combat sport involving grappling techniques: clinching, throws, takedowns and pins.

Down:

1.A fast paced indoor sport played on a table, players use small bats to hit a light ball.

2.A sport that involves horseback disciplines such as dressage and show jumping.

Across:

2.A collection of sporting events: track and field, running, jumping and throwing.

3.The sport of shooting arrows with a bow, typically at a target for accuracy.

Down:

1.Played on a rectangle court, players aim to shoot a ball through a hoop.

4.A sport where individuals or teams propel boats through water using oars.

ANSWERS

					4 T		
2 B	a	s	e	b	a	l	l
					e		
		1 H	o	c	k	e	y
					w		
					o		
3 S	u	r	f	i	n	g	
					d		
					o		

Taekwondo
Baseball
Hockey
Surfing

ANSWERS

	1 U	S	3 A			5 G
			r			e
			g			r
			e			m
4 C	h	i	n	a		a
			t			n
			i			y
2 F	r	a	n	c	e	
			a			

USA
Argentina
China
France
Germany

ANSWERS

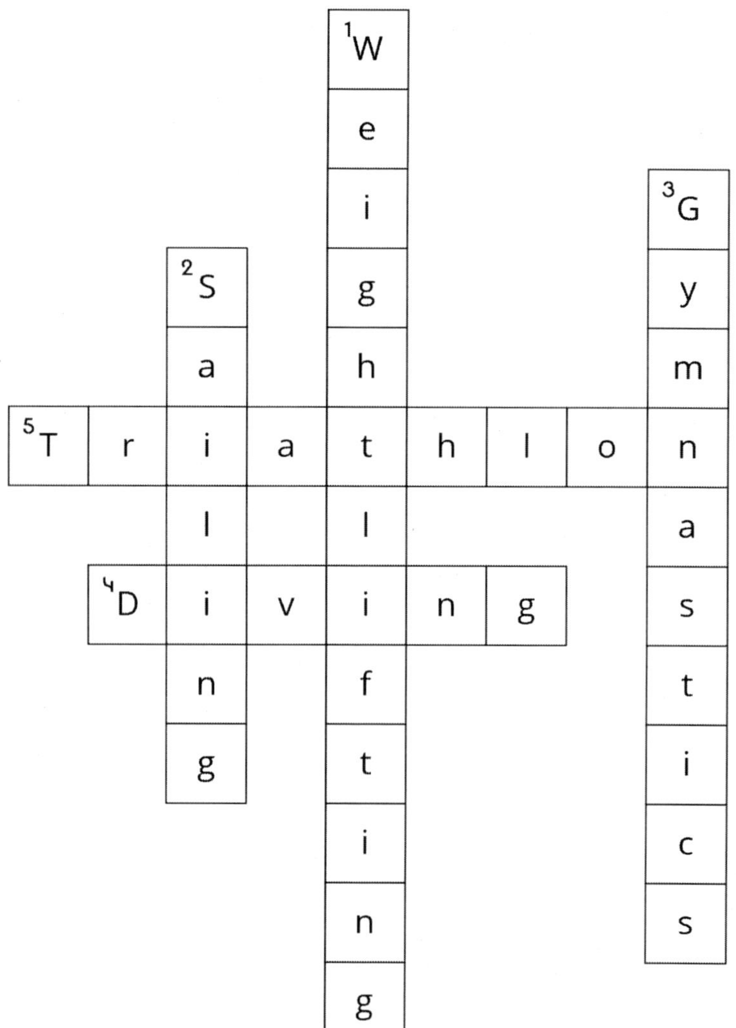

Sailing
Triathlon
Diving
Weight-lifting
Gymnastics

ANSWERS

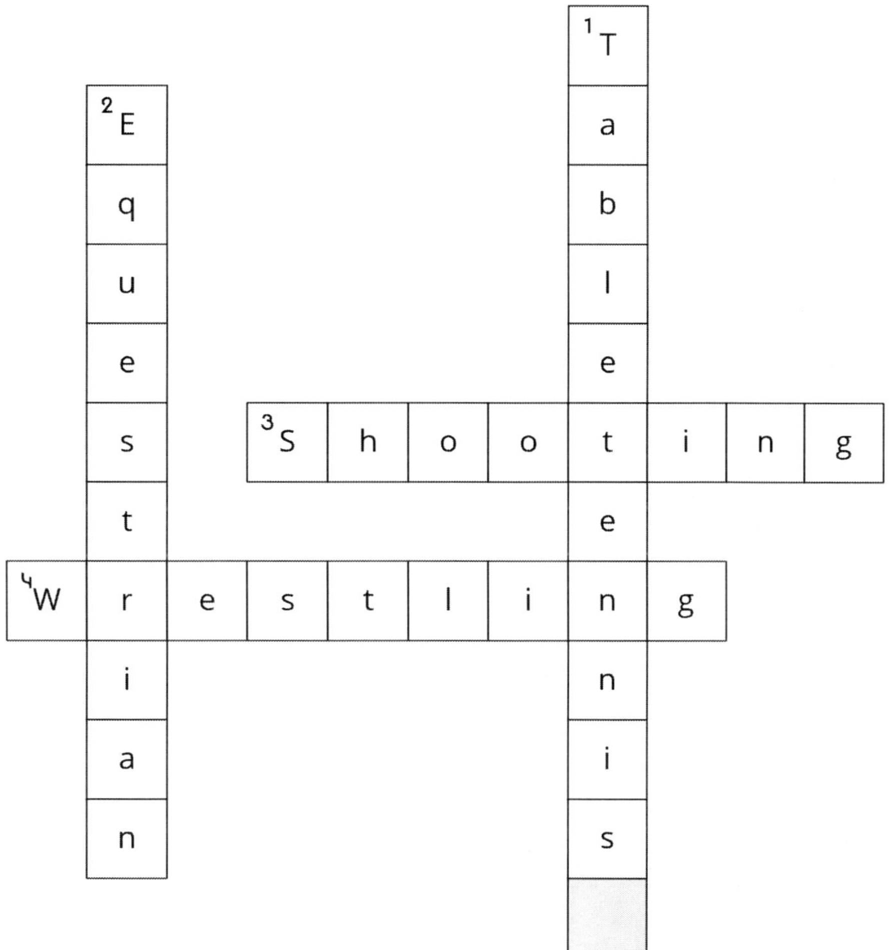

Equestrian
Wrestling
Shooting
Table-tennis

ANSWERS

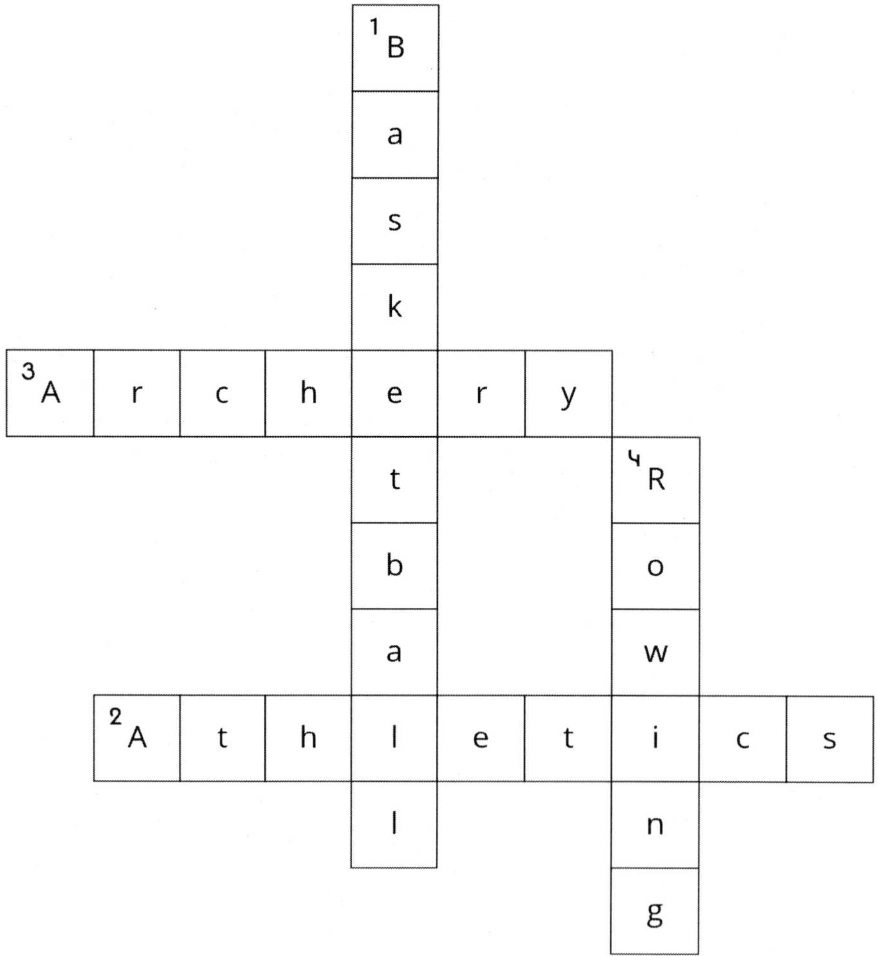

Basketball
Archery
Athletics
Rowing

History round:

What event marked the revival of the Olympic Games in the modern era?

A) The lighting of the Olympic flame in Olympia, Greece
B) The first ancient Olympic Games in Olympia, Greece
C) The unveiling of the Olympic rings
D) The 1896 Olympics in Athens, Greece

How is the Olympia flame lit before every Olympic Games?

A) Using a torch
B) Using a match
C) Using the sun's rays
D) Using electricity

What do the five Olympic rings symbolize?

A) The five senses
B) The five inhabited continents of the world
C) The five elements
D) The five Olympic mascots

Which animal was the first Olympic mascot?

A) Tiger
B) Lion
C) Dachshund
D) Elephant

When were the first ancient Olympic Games held?

A) 500 BCE
B) 776 CE
C) 1896 CE
D) 100 AD

What is the motto of the Olympic Games?

A) "Unity in Diversity"
B) "Stronger Together"
C) "Citius, Altius, Fortius"
D) "Peace and Friendship"

In which city were the first modern Olympic Games held?

A) Paris, France
B) Rome, Italy
C) Athens, Greece
D) London, England

Which ancient Greek god was the Olympic Games originally held in honour of?

A) Zeus
B) Athena
C) Poseidon
D) Apollo

Score: /8

Athletes & Sport round:

Who holds the record for the most Olympic gold medals won by an individual athlete?

A) Simone Biles
B) Michael Phelps
C) Usain Bolt
D) Tom Daley

Which athlete became famous for representing Great Britain in ski jumping at the 1988 Winter Olympics?

A) Michael Phelps
B) Usain Bolt
C) Eddie "The Eagle" Edwards
D) Yuzuru Hanyu

Who is considered the fastest man in the world and holds the world record for the fastest 100-meter and 200-meter sprints?

A) Justin Gatlin
B) Simone Biles
C) Usain Bolt
D) Katie Ledecky

How many Olympic gold medals did Michael Phelps win during his career?

A) 10
B) 15
C) 20
D) 23

In which sport did Michael Phelps win most of his Olympic gold medals?

A) Swimming
B) Track and field
C) Gymnastics
D) Ski jumping

What is Usain Bolt's nationality?

A) Jamaican
B) American
C) British
D) Canadian

Who is the American gymnast known for her record-breaking medal hauls at the World Championships?

A) Gabby Douglas
B) Michael Phelps
C) Simone Biles
D) Yuzuru Hanyu

Which American track and field athlete won four gold medals at the 1984 Los Angeles Olympics, matching the record set in 1936?

A) Carl Lewis
B) Jackie Joyner-Kersee
C) Florence Griffith-Joyner
D) Michael Johnson

Score: /8

Olympic symbols:

What does the Olympic torch relay symbolise?

A) The passing of the Olympic torch from one generation to the next
B) The beginning of the Olympic Games
C) The end of the Olympic Games
D) The victory of the Olympic athletes

What is the meaning of the Olympic motto "Citius, Altius, Fortius"?

A) "Unity in Diversity"
B) "Faster, Higher, Stronger"
C) "Peace and Friendship"
D) "Excellence in Sportsmanship"

Who composed the Olympic anthem played during the opening ceremonies of the Olympics?

A) Ludwig van Beethoven
B) Johann Sebastian Bach
C) Spyridon Samaras
D) Wolfgang Amadeus Mozart

Who takes the Olympic oath during the opening ceremonies of the Olympics?

A) The president of the International Olympic Committee
B) A athlete representing the competitors, A judge, and a coach
C) The host country's head of state
D) The captain of the host country's Olympic team

What is the significance of the Olympic rings?

A) They represent unity of the five continents participating
B) They represent the five elements of nature
C) They symbolise the five Olympic values
D) They represent the five main Olympic sports

What do the opening and closing ceremonies of the Olympics showcase?

A) The first event
B) The history of the Olympic Games
C) The host country's culture and heritage
D) The future of the Olympic movement

Where were the most recent Olympic Games held?

A) Tokyo, Japan
B) Rio de Janeiro, Brazil
C) Beijing, China
D) Pyeongchang, South Korea

What are the five colours of the Olympic rings?

A) Red, Yellow, Green, Blue, Purple
B) Orange, Yellow, Green, Blue, Red
C) Pink, Purple, Blue, Green, Yellow
D) Blue, Red, Green, Yellow, Black

Score: /8

Culture round:

How is the host city for each Olympic Games selected?

A) Through a random drawing
B) By popular vote on social media
C) By the International Olympic Committee through a bidding process
D) By the host country's government

Which country hosted the Olympic Games in 2008?

A) France
B) Japan
C) China
D) Australia

What is the purpose of the Olympic Village?

A) To showcase cultural performances
B) To house athletes during the Games
C) To host the opening and closing ceremonies
D) To serve as a training facility for athletes

What is one way the host city showcases its culture during the Olympics?

A) By hosting international trade fairs
B) By organising political debates
C) Through performances at the opening and closing ceremonies
D) By constructing new shopping malls

Which event immediately follows the Olympic Games?

A) The World Cup
B) The Paralympic Games
C) The Super Bowl
D) The FIFA World Championships

What is the Olympic Truce?

A) A period of time when all Olympic events are postponed
B) D) A competition between Olympic host cities
C) A treaty signed by all participating countries before the Games
D) Ancient tradition calling for a cessation of hostilities during the Olympic Games

What legacy do the Olympic Games leave in host cities?

A) Improved infrastructure and facilities
B) New shopping malls
C) Increased pollution
D) Higher crime rates

Who organizes the Paralympic Games?

A) The International Paralympic Committee
B) The International Olympic Committee
C) The United Nations
D) The host city's government

Score: /8

ANSWERS

History round:

D, B, D, C, B, C, C, A

Athletes & Sport round:

B, C, C, D, A, A, C, A

ANSWERS

Olympic symbols:

A, B, C, B, A, C, A, D

Culture round:

C, C, B, C, B, D, A, A

Made in United States
North Haven, CT
02 August 2024

55671508R00046